SIR ISAAC NEWTON

FERNANDO GORDON

Consulting Editor, Diane Craig, M.A./Reading Specialist

Super Sandcastle

An Imprint of Abdo Publishing
abdopublishing.com

abdopublishing.com

Printed in the United States of America, North Mankato, Minnesota
062016
092016

THIS BOOK CONTAINS
RECYCLED MATERIALS

Editor: Rebecca Felix
Content Developer: Nancy Tuminelly
Cover and Interior Design and Production: Mighty Media, Inc.
Photo Credits: iStockphoto; Shutterstock; Wellcome Library, London; Wikimedia Commons

Library of Congress Cataloging-in-Publication Data
Names: Gordon, Fernando, author.
Title: Sir Isaac Newton / by Fernando Gordon ; consulting editor, Diane
  Craig, M.A./reading specialist.
Description: Minneapolis, Minnesota : Abdo Publishing, [2017] | Series:
  Scientists at work
Identifiers: LCCN 2016001423 (print) | LCCN 2016005193 (ebook) | ISBN
  9781680781588 (print) | ISBN 9781680776010 (ebook)
Subjects: LCSH: Newton, Isaac, 1642-1727--Juvenile literature. |
  Physicists--Great Britain--Biography--Juvenile literature. |
  Scientists--Great Britain--Biography--Juvenile literature. |
  Physics--History--Juvenile literature.
Classification: LCC QC16.N7 G594 2017 (print) | LCC QC16.N7 (ebook) | DDC
  530.092--dc23
LC record available at http://lccn.loc.gov/2016001423 4841

Super SandCastle™ books are created by a team of professional educators, reading specialists, and content developers around five essential components—phonemic awareness, phonics, vocabulary, text comprehension, and fluency—to assist young readers as they develop reading skills and strategies and increase their general knowledge. All books are written, reviewed, and leveled for guided reading, early reading intervention, and Accelerated Reader™ programs for use in shared, guided, and independent reading and writing activities to support a balanced approach to literacy instruction.

CONTENTS

MARVELOUS MATHEMATICIAN

Sir Isaac Newton was a famous scientist. He was a **mathematician** too. He created many **theories**.

Sir Isaac Newton

ISAAC NEWTON

BORN: December 25, 1642, Woolsthorpe, England

MARRIED: never married

CHILDREN: none

DIED: March 20, 1727, London, England

FARM LIFE

Isaac Newton was born on a farm in England.

Isaac went to school in his youth. But he had to quit before finishing. His family needed his help on the farm.

But Isaac hated farm life. He did not like doing chores. Instead he read books. Finally, Isaac's family let him go back to school.

Isaac's family farm in Woolsthorpe, England

COLLEGE

Newton left home in 1661. He moved to Cambridge, England. He went to Trinity College to study science.

Newton was very curious. He read many books. He took notes on what he read. He thought about science's unanswered questions.

Trinity College in Cambridge, England

TRAGEDY AND DISCOVERY

Newton graduated in 1665. He hoped to teach at the college. But that same year, **tragedy** hit nearby London. A deadly illness killed many people. Trinity College was shut down.

The illness, known as the Great Plague, killed many people across Europe.

Newton went back home. There, he read and studied. He wrote **theories**. He also made many discoveries.

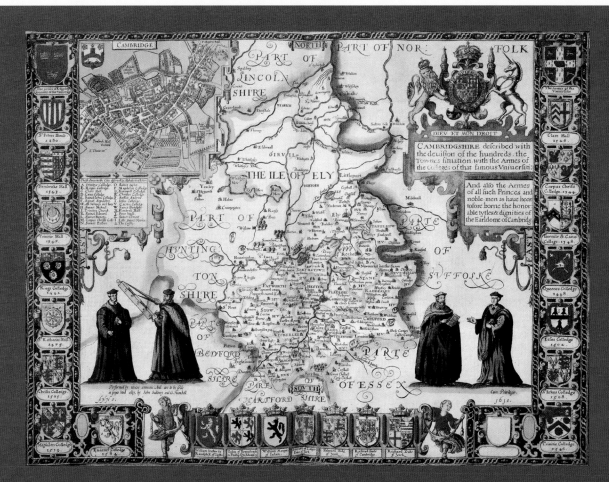

A map of Cambridge and Cambridgeshire county in the 1600s

GRAVITY

Newton discovered gravity. But not everyone agrees on how. One telling of the story says Newton got the idea from an apple.

Newton saw an apple fall from a tree. He knew objects at rest remain at rest.

This apple tree is on Newton's family farm. Newton may have been sitting under it when the famous apple fell.

That means they do not move unless pushed by a force. Newton realized an unseen force was at work! It was gravity. It pulled on the apple. This made it fall!

An apple tree planted in Cambridge. This tree is said to be from the seeds of Newton's famous apple tree.

MATHEMATICS

Trinity College reopened in 1667. Newton went back to school. By then, he had become a well-known **mathematician**. He had written about a new kind of math. It was called "the calculus."

Isaac Barrow was the college's head math professor. He was **impressed** by Newton's work.

In 1669, Barrow thought Newton should take his place. Newton became a professor.

Isaac Barrow

CHALLENGES

OPTICKS:

OR, A

TREATISE

OF THE

REFLEXIONS, REFRACTIONS,

INFLEXIONS and COLOURS

OF

LIGHT.

ALSO

Two TREATISES

OF THE

SPECIES and MAGNITUDE

OF

Curvilinear Figures.

LONDON,

Printed for SAM. SMITH, and BENJ. WALFORD,
Printers to the Royal Society, at the Prince's Arms in
St. Paul's Church-yard. MDCCIV.

Newton taught his math **theories**. He worked on science theories too. He wrote a book about his ideas on light. It is called *Opticks*.

A first edition of Newton's book on light theories

Newton did many experiments with light.

In 1672, a light **expert** read *Opticks*. His name was Robert Hooke. Hooke **criticized** Newton's ideas. Newton was very upset. He went into hiding for years.

LAWS OF MOTION

In 1679, Newton and Hooke exchanged letters. They argued about laws of motion. Newton wanted to show that Hooke was wrong. So he proved a new set of laws.

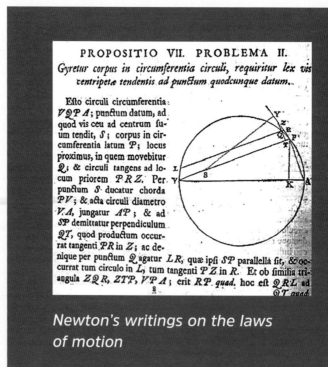

Newton's writings on the laws of motion

He wrote them down in a book called *Principia*. It was published in 1687. Its Three Laws of Motion are the basis of **physics.** They explain how mass, force, and **inertia** affect an object's movement.

PHILOSOPHIÆ
NATURALIS
PRINCIPIA
MATHEMATICA.

Autore JS. NEWTON, Trin. Coll. Cantab. Soc. Matheseos Professore Lucasiano, & Societatis Regalis Sodali.

IMPRIMATUR.
S. PEPYS, Reg. Soc. PRÆSES.
Julii 5. 1686.

LONDINI,
Jussu Societatis Regiæ ac Typis Josephi Streater. Prostat apud plures Bibliopolas. Anno MDCLXXXVII.

NEWTON'S IMPACT

Newton saw many challenges in life. But he saw much success too. He created many **theories**. Many are still studied today.

Newton lived to the age of 84.

Newton was one of history's most important scientists. His ideas changed the way people understand light, gravity, and motion.

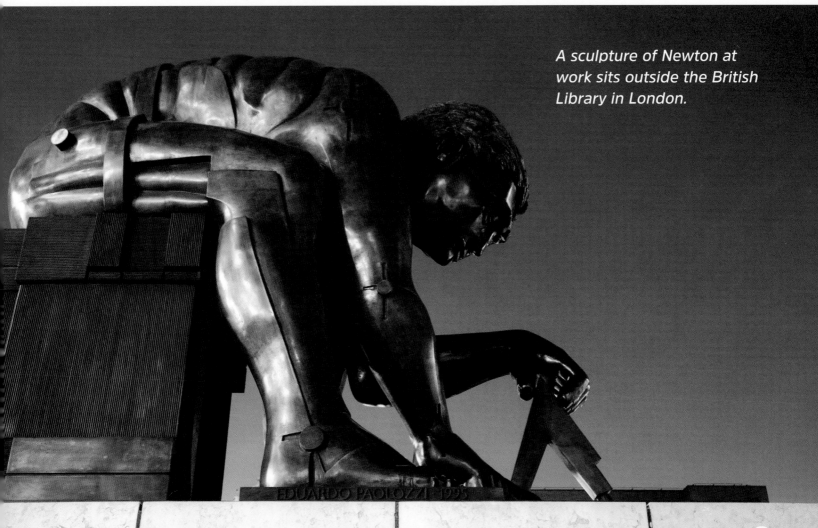

A sculpture of Newton at work sits outside the British Library in London.

MORE ABOUT NEWTON

Newton was born VERY SMALL. Doctors weren't sure he would live.

The Queen of England made Newton a KNIGHT in 1705. This is why "Sir" is added to his name.

As a child, Newton built CLOCKS and other MACHINES.

TEST YOUR KNOWLEDGE

1. Newton went to Trinity College.
True or false?

2. What was Newton's book *Opticks* about?

3. How many laws of motion did Newton come up with?

THINK ABOUT IT!

Where do you see motion at work?

ANSWERS: 1. True 2. Light 3. Three

GLOSSARY

criticize – to state that a person is doing something wrong.

expert – a person very knowledgeable about a certain subject.

impress – to get someone's attention or interest.

inertia – a law of physics. It says a resting object tends to stay at rest and a moving object tends to stay in motion.

mathematician – a math expert.

physics – the science of how energy and objects affect each other.

theory – an idea that explains how or why something happens.

tragedy – a very sad and surprising event.